PAINTING KATRINA

PAINTING KATRINA

PHIL SANDUSKY

PELICAN PUBLISHING COMPANY

GRETNA 2007

To all the people whose lives were ravaged by the hurricanes of 2005, to the first responders and volunteers who put themselves in harm's way to save lives, to the private citizens from all walks of life and all parts of the country who gave us shelter and helped us rebuild, and to the indomitable spirit of our beautiful New Orleans

The word "Pelican" and the depiction of a pelican are trademarks of Pelican Publishing Company, Inc., and are registered in the U.S. Patent and Trademark Office.

Library of Congress Cataloging-in-Publication Data

Sandusky, Phil.
  Painting Katrina / Phil Sandusky.
    p. cm.
  ISBN 978-1-58980-477-7 (hardcover : alk. paper) 1. Sandusky, Phil--Catalogs. 2. New Orleans (La.)--In art--Catalogs. 3. Hurricane Katrina, 2005--Pictorial works. I. Title.
  ND237.S277A4 2007
  759.13--dc22

                                    2007016924

Printed in Singapore
Published by Pelican Publishing Company, Inc.
1000 Burmaster Street, Gretna, Louisiana 70053

PAINTING KATRINA

Camp and Marengo streets, June 2006. 18" x 24". (All paintings shown in this book were done in oil paint on canvas or canvas board.)

In this book I will show you landscape paintings I produced in New Orleans prior to and after Hurricane Katrina and share my journal of experiences painting the hurricane destruction. I work exclusively on location (*en plein air*), and each painting is completed in a single sitting. I include paintings of New Orleans before Katrina because I will not present a view of New Orleans decimated by Katrina without also showing you a view of the city in better times. I have not endeavored to make post-Katrina paintings of specific subjects that I had previously painted so that before-and-after views could be compared. I wanted to portray the damage done to New Orleans as effectively as possible and therefore my post-Katrina subjects were selected based on their own merits. Given that specific subjects and vantage points within these two bodies of work are different, what comparisons can really be drawn? Perhaps none, if your goals are forensic. However, the overall effect of a painting, its mood, and the way it conveys a state of mind are more important than its subject. Order versus chaos, happy versus sad, calm versus violent, mundane versus dramatic are qualities best expressed when not concerned with following a restrictive, before-and-after motif. I believe that you will find the contrasts between the views of New Orleans seen through my pre-Katrina eyes and those seen through my post-Katrina eyes to be meaningful and truthful.

There have been certain expressionist and surrealist painters who would paint an ordinary, happy, suburban neighborhood to make it look as though it had been hellishly churned up in a blender. They bend the subject matter to communicate their own angst about life in general. I wonder how they would have painted the firebombing of Dresden or the aftermath of the eruption of Mount Vesuvius in Pompeii . . . or the devastation of Hurricane Katrina in the Lower Ninth Ward. I want to tell the simple truth about what I see. Admittedly, I am not a photorealist, meticulously copying the image. I create an image on the canvas that is designed to show you what I see. What I see is different from what a lifeless reproduction of the image could convey. I try to capture the poetry and the essence of the thing in the same way that our senses do. The mind is like the CEO of a large company. The CEO doesn't want to see raw data. He doesn't want to know the details of every specific transaction made at each district office. He wants to be presented with trends, graphs, summaries, and how this year's numbers compare with last year's. Similarly, the mind is ill equipped to handle the raw data gathered by the photoreceptors in our eyes. It wants to see how this data is ordered. It wants to see how colors are different from each other, not what colors are there. It wants to see how forms resonate to make shapes, and how these shapes and color relationships compare to those from previous experiences. It wants to see how a thing goes from narrow to wide or smooth to ragged. It doesn't count how many cinderblocks are present in a debris field but wants to know if there are many or few and revels in *how* they are scattered. This is the essence of poetry . . . the higher order of things. This is what we see and experience, not the raw image.

In every situation, but especially in post-Katrina New Orleans, where the physical chaos is visually and emotionally overwhelming, the effect of the firsthand experience is too big, the light is too strong, and there is too much busyness to copy every detail of it onto a canvas and have it be effective or, in some cases, even make any sense. As an artist, I want to present you with the distilled essence of the thing. I will do this not by intensifying the level of destruction in these post-Katrina paintings but by abstracting and simplifying it, as our senses do. I will show the order in it, to make you feel what I feel when I'm standing there taking it in firsthand.

Though my paintings are simplified and quickly done, they give the illusion of being complex. It is amazing how well your mind can fill in the details. In fact, it is more satisfying and meaningful to have the details pulled up from the depth of your subconscious mind than spoon-fed to you by a sharply focused photograph. Ultimately, my paintings look just like what I am painting. People who see me painting on location tell me so, and I want to be held accountable for it. I title my paintings for the locations where they were done. Most of the devastated structures I painted have already been razed. But, rest assured, this is what they looked like when I first saw them.

I've been painting in New Orleans since 1985. It was here that I essentially discovered landscape painting. Before I came to New Orleans I was predominantly a studio painter, working from the figure and still life. I occasionally ventured out to do landscape painting, but my efforts were meager. I did it only as an exercise, thinking that it would expand my skills. I never really connected with it or had a passion for it. This would change when I came to New Orleans. When I arrived, I fell in love with the city's European flavor, unique architecture, and lush flora. This newfound love might have been enough in itself to compel me to do some serious landscape painting, but another issue also helped awaken me to this genre. I had become disenchanted with my style of painting.

Over the years, the excitement that I felt as a student, exploring what I saw with paint, had slowly given way to an arduous, painful process of making beautiful pictures. (In retrospect they weren't very beautiful.) I had come to realize that, in developing paintings in the studio over many sittings, I had also developed a cumbersome, iterative, indirect process of painting. This process had become so big that I had become lost in it and subservient to it. I looked for subjects that I thought it would like and feared its retribution if I did not faithfully apply every one of its formulae. I began to see through its eyes. A demon such as this creeps into an artist's studio like mold. It is fed by a lack of urgency. A still-life arrangement doesn't move, and the lighting never changes. I had all the time in the world to ponder it and revise my painting of it again and again, in the belief that I was making it prettier and prettier. I had plenty of time to become fearful of messing up what I had accomplished after a couple of sittings, so that only delicate, timid changes could be made to the painting over the next several sittings. There was also plenty of time to become so immured in the universe of the canvas, spending countless hours looking at it, that any ability that I had to see it objectively was lost. It seemed that I had become paralyzed by time and fear.

During this period of disillusionment, while visiting an art museum I came across a painting by the post-impressionist Maurice de Vlaminck. Never having cared too much for the Fauves, I initially gave it no more than a passing glance. But something about this painting haunted me as I explored the rest of the collection. I returned to look at it again and was struck by a singular truth. Vlaminck had fun painting it! I had seen many other paintings that day that I liked much better and I'm certain the artists who did those paintings had every bit as much fun as Vlaminck. But I suppose I had to see a painting where this was the only quality that I liked about it to realize that this most important quality was missing from my own work. It was then that I decided to paint more simply and directly, to return to my student days of honestly showing people what I see. I would no longer be concerned with making beautiful, tasteful paintings. Most of all I would have fun! From that point on I began to do brushy, loose, one-sitting paintings. I continued to paint from the figure and still life in my studio, but using this new approach, and I also began to seriously attack landscape painting.

I was amazed to discover how little brainpower I had been using with my old, indirect process. With the old process, a painting was done in many steps, each providing a crutch for the next: first the drawing, then the values, then the delicate transitions to color. In fact, time itself was used as a crutch. With my new, direct process, I had to grasp the subject at once as a whole, see all of the patterns that composed it, and formulate and follow through with a course of action to set them down upon the canvas. At the end of a painting session I felt exhausted, as though I had taken a very difficult test. It is amazing how much better a draftsman you become when you don't draw before you paint, and how "beautiful and tasteful" a painting is that simply succeeds in showing people what you see. I had reinvented myself as a direct painter. A direct painter's process can turn on a dime. He does not see in terms of his process, as an indirect painter does. Rather, his process is steered to serve what *he* sees. He has a significant visual experience that he wants to convey. He visualizes a set of patterns sitting next to and on top of each other in the picture plane. He formulates a plan to place those patterns onto the canvas, and then acts. It's just that simple! The mystery, depth, substance, and soul lie more in the seeing and less in the process. Freed from my duties as a frazzled servant to my indirect process of painting, I was able to concern myself more with the science of seeing. When your application of paint is brash and simple, your vision must be profound. And what could be more important? How could I have lost track of this over the years? I had been swimming through thick molasses! Before, I was trying to hunt rabbits with a Sherman tank. Now I became nimble and light, focused and attuned to my environment, like Daniel Boone with his trusty Kentucky long rifle.

I am lucky that my first ventures into landscape painting in New Orleans coincided with this change in my process. I come from an artistic lineage insistent upon working only from the live subject. Not only is the firsthand experience infinitely richer than looking at a photo, but the limitations and challenges of working from life make the artist stronger. This mandate would necessitate that I work only *en plein air* when doing my landscape painting. With the fugitive conditions outdoors, such as constantly changing light and sky and parked vehicles driving away, I can only imagine the lifeless, dreary landscape paintings of New Orleans I would have produced had I executed them with my "pre-Vlaminck" process. I most likely would have lost interest. As it was, my new approach seemed to be made for plein-air landscape painting.

My initial attempts were crude. But it felt good to be going in a different direction, breaking old habits and painting from a new subject. After a few months I was doing the best painting I had ever done. I was hooked on landscape painting.

Nationally and internationally, there has been a resurgence of plein-air painting in recent years. Its very name gives testament to this. When I began to paint outdoors in New Orleans in the 1980s, I and the few others who did it referred to it as "landscape painting." When talking to the unindoctrinated, I called it "doing landscape painting on location from the live subject." At that time, "plein air," which, happily, has fewer syllables, was an antiquated term known by most representational artists but seldom used. It was used more in the nineteenth and early twentieth centuries. As late as 1995 it was still uncommon. At that time I was interviewed on a radio talk show by an art professor who introduced me to the audience as "an easel painter": "he *actually* puts a canvas on an easel, looks at something, and paints what he sees." I felt like a duck-billed platypus. I'm not sure exactly when the term "plein air" became commonly used to categorize what I do, but it certainly corresponded to a renewed interest in painting outdoors. In the 1980s I hardly ever saw an easel outdoors in New Orleans. When I did, I knew the person standing behind it. People who saw me painting outside thought I was an escapee from Jackson Square. Once during this time when I was painting in City Park, I was distracted by a clacking sound coming from the back of my sketch box. I peered around my canvas to discover that an old man walking back to his tour bus had deposited a handful of change. He must have thought, "The poor guy probably doesn't have a place to live, much less a camera, otherwise why would he be standing out here doing this in the heat?" Now I see easels often and seldom know the artists. People have discovered how pleasurable and satisfying it is to paint outdoors. However, there are still very few professional landscape painters who work exclusively *en plein air*.

Today professional artists use plein-air painting mostly to make preliminary studies from which, along with photographic references, larger, more elaborate works will be made over many sittings in the studio. These preparatory, plein-air sketches capture a few, big notes of color, but the artist has no expectation that they will fully communicate his or her point of view. They are but a part of the artist's overall process, though an important part, in that they remind the artist of the gist of the subject as he delves into the details. The larger, articulated studio piece is made because the artist wants to make a painting that he believes will have more presence and provide more information about many facets of the subject. There is also great pressure on artists to make more monumental paintings. There are many exceptionally talented artists who are quite successful with this approach. Their initial plein-air studies are thought of by the public as "quaint" and "charming" and their larger end result is thought of as "majestic" and "breathtaking."

But do single-sitting, plein-air paintings have to exist solely in this "quaint" and "charming" realm? Bigger isn't necessarily better, and more detail, while providing more information, seldom produces a painting that is as strong as a whole as does a well-done sketch. One has only to think of great painters such as Sargent, Sorolla, and Monet to be reminded that plein-air painting can succeed in and of itself. Their work was not good *considering* that it was done *en plein air;* it was good *because* it was done *en plein air.* And they did not limit the size of their plein-air paintings to petite, nine-by-twelve-inch panels. I believe that great things can come from setting our expectations higher for what can be accomplished working quickly, succinctly, and exclusively from the live subject.

What advantages, if any, could be gained by working quickly, outdoors in adverse conditions and changing light? How could a painting produced in this way be better in any respect than one done in multiple sittings, in the controlled environment of the studio? Many landscape painters would say that on-site studies are important because human eyes discern subtle differences in color much better than any current photographic technology. This is true, but is merely the tip of the iceberg. There are several other ways in which plein-air painting excels.

First and most important, paintings that are done quickly and gesturally from life tend to be better aligned with real, human vision. As we glance at our subject, we don't see every detail as a photograph does. We see the big picture. We only notice individual parts insofar as how they interrelate to form the whole. When our attention is pulled into a smaller part, that becomes the whole, with even smaller parts forming it, and our perception of it is altered. The first principle of Gestalt, which is the single most important principle of visual perception, states that "the whole is different from the sum of its parts." This means that when we look at one object in a scene (such as a shrub), move our eyes around it and assess it, and then move our eyes over to another object (such as a car), and focus all attention on it, and then another and so forth, the sum total of all these different experiences is not the same as the experience we have when we move our eyes around the entire larger view. One-sitting, plein-air painting aligns itself with this principle better than any other form of painting. The artist, thrust into the immense, constantly changing torrents of nature, is unable to focus all attention on each part separately, as he might be able to do with a multisitting studio painting. He must grasp the subject as a whole at an instant in time. By necessity, he must state the parts more simply as they appear, while his attention remains on the bigger view. This is why nicely done, one-sitting sketches usually look better as a whole when viewed from a distance than do larger, more articulated studio pieces. It is why Constable's sketches are vibrant and crisp and evoke a sense that we are in his head, looking out through his eyes, while his larger, articulated studio pieces are nicely done, but lifeless, renderings of the same scenes.

Second, the sketchiness of quickly executed paintings gives great insight into the artist's process. There is no time to repeatedly rework and polish areas of the canvas, so, on close inspection, we can see remnants of the underpainting and how patterns were placed on top of it. We can see evidence of the artist's initial conceptualization of the piece in the finished work. We can see the artist's hand in the work. There is a beauty in the way an artist's understanding of what he sees, and of painting in general, rises above the limitations imposed by working quickly from the live subject.

Yet another advantage that plein-air painting has over studio painting lies in the immediacy of it. We should not underestimate the effect that our past visual memories have upon what we see in the present moment. Even as we glance around a scene, as our center of vision shifts from one place to another, our memory of the part of our view on which we were last focused has already begun to be transformed by our lifetime collection of visual memories. This is not a bad thing unless we allow what we see and paint to become too generalized. This flavoring of a raw image with our visual memories constitutes our individual point of view. It is our very reason for painting. However, it has been shown that very shortly after we see something, most of our memories of its specific nuances have dissolved into the well of our lifetime of visual memories. Working quickly from the live subject is the best way to preserve these nuances and the specific nature of a visual experience (although, some of my colleagues would prefer photos!).

What's more, decisions about composition, pattern, and color are not necessarily improved by extensive contemplation in the studio. Some of the best artistic decisions can be made quickly and intuitively. Decisions that are ruminated over for a long time tend to be more formulaic and safe. In fact, when there is more time, decisions tend to be compartmentalized into separate aspects or parts of the piece, producing a less integrated result. It's amazing what great decisions can be made

when you understand that this one moment is the freshest and fullest this vision will ever be in your mind. You don't have a 35mm lifeboat to depend on. You feel your brain creak and groan like a U-boat that's gone a little too deep. This is not to say that decisions made quickly are always good. Artists who make single-sitting paintings from life and have lofty goals about what they want to accomplish are prone to fail often. Speaking for myself, 75 percent of the paintings I do are unsuccessful and therefore wiped off so that the canvases can be recycled. Yet when I succeed there is a unique power in my work that can only be attributed to working quickly and succinctly from the firsthand experience, *en plein air.*

If this resurgence of plein-air painting should ever constitute a new art movement in the third millennium, I can only hope that it will not be sold short by having as its icon a quaint, charming little thing that has to be elaborated upon in the studio. Let's set the bar high. Great things can be done in the changing sun!

JOURNAL

I drove away from New Orleans, caravanning two cars with my wife, mother-in-law, two dogs, and three cats. We left town, as did so many other people, expecting to return in a couple of days. I haven't spoken to any early evacuees of Katrina who didn't sit transfixed, as we did, in front of the television in the first few days following the storm, watching the catastrophe unfold on CNN. We were disoriented for some time, uncertain as to when we would be able to return, or if we would have anything to return to. I can only imagine the mental state of those who stayed in New Orleans, rode out the storm, and evacuated after it passed.

In the following days we began to get our bearings. Our attention turned towards our personal finances. Even though we were staying with my parents in Jacksonville, Florida we still had bills to pay. My wife, a clinical social worker with the

Louisiana State University Department of Psychiatry, was called back to New Orleans about a week after the storm passed to help coordinate a mental-health support program for first responders. She was given a special pass to enter the city and resided on one of the cruise ships that had been provided for first responders. It would be at least a month before the general population would be allowed to return. I was concerned that the art market in New Orleans would be diminished in the short term, so I used this time to cultivate other markets for my painting outside of New Orleans. First, I was able to do a considerable amount of plein-air painting of Atlanta's majestic, urban landscape, something I had been meaning to do for a long time. I stayed with my good friends (and New Orleans expatriates) the Reinikes of the Reinike Gallery, who represent me in Atlanta. While I was there, they organized an impromptu hurricane-relief benefit exhibit at the gallery, which was very successful.

When residents of my zip code were allowed reentry, I returned to New Orleans for about a week to do some basic remediation of my own damaged house. We were lucky to live in a part of town that didn't flood, but unluckily we had severe roof damage from Katrina, which allowed the heavy rains of Hurricane Rita to enter our house. After clearing away what seemed to be 2,000 pounds of sweet gum tree from on and around my house, tarping the roof, and handling some basic mold abatement, I was off to Jacksonville once again.

I enlisted a gallery to represent me there (Stellers Gallery), stocked them with many paintings that I had done on previous trips to Jacksonville, and spent a couple of weeks doing some more paintings for them. During this second trip to Jacksonville, I grew anxious to get back to New Orleans so that I could capture the devastation caused by the hurricane before it could be cleaned up. I have been known in the region as one of the leading painterly documentarians of New Orleans' neighborhoods and architecture. I felt it would be a shame if I didn't produce a significant body of work that captured the effects of the worst natural disaster to strike the city, the region, and indeed, the nation.

As I drove back to New Orleans, my artistic needs struggled with my practical needs. I realized that I would have to budget time to both capture the hurricane devastation on canvas and get my own house back together. I decided that I would paint in the morning and work on my house in the afternoon. While I would spend less time painting than usual, the time I did spend would be unfettered by guilt about neglecting my personal problems.

My first ventures out to paint the effects of Katrina were to a section of town called Mid-City, about a ten-minute drive from my house. Most days I went with my good friend and painting buddy, Diego Larguia (one of his paintings is shown on page 18). It was greatly reassuring to not have to venture out solo at this time, because there was still talk about such things as gangs of looters and packs of wild, hungry dogs. Diego and I are both lucky to live in the part of town closest to the Mississippi River. This "sliver along the river" extends from Uptown (where I live) through the Irish Channel (where Diego lives), Garden District, Warehouse District, French Quarter, Marigny, and Bywater neighborhoods. It was formed as part of the river's natural levee and is the oldest, settled part of New Orleans. The land in these parts of town can be as much as twelve feet above sea level.

Less than a mile from my Uptown neighborhood, as we drove away from the high ground near the river towards Mid-City, we saw the ominous, dirty waterline begin to appear on the foundations of the houses and buildings. This water line slowly rose as we descended deeper into the bowl. Debris littered the streets, limiting access to many areas.

Turning off the main avenue into the first navigable Mid-City street we could find, I initially felt a little guilty, as though we didn't have the right to be there. It also seemed dangerous. There was a sour smell in the air, and debris was everywhere. If a street was cleared, it was only to a width of one lane in the middle of the road. Upturned roofing nails in or out of shingles seemed to be the biggest hazard for the car.

Each time we set up to paint, in Mid-City as well as other places over the next few weeks, I always had an uneasy feeling that we were going to be run off at any moment. There were many officials, workers wearing hard hats and carrying clipboards, and National Guardsmen. As it turned out, these people tiptoed around us (when not driving a front-loader or Humvee) and treated us with an almost inappropriate respect. I discovered later that most of them were from out of state and considered all residents of New Orleans, whether from this particular neighborhood or not, to be victims. The New Orleans police, tired and overworked, were only concerned about preventing looting and didn't seem to be worried about a couple of guys painting. In fact, sometimes they took an interest in what we were doing and advised us as to where we might find some even more dramatic views. The Lower Ninth Ward came up often, but at that time entry was limited to emergency workers. Streets there were impassable, and bodies were still being recovered.

What we found in Mid-City was very dense sediment covering everything that had been flooded. Though the floodwater was much deeper in other parts of the city, in retrospect it must have been dirtiest here, perhaps because it traveled farther inland over the gritty urban landscape. Most compelling visually was the way this dense sediment covered the cars. There were stratification lines on the sediment-covered vehicles showing where the water level had risen and lowered, staying stagnant at certain levels for longer periods of time. It reminded me of the stratification that can be seen in certain rocks, a process that happens in geological time, whereas this floodwater sedimentation happened over only days or weeks. While there was a significant amount of debris from the wind and slow-moving floodwater, much of the debris was tattered drywall and appliances from the few neighborhood residents who had already returned to clean out their houses. Artistically, it was challenging to state this debris convincingly. My first attempts made it look more like popcorn or confetti. Eventually I found that articulating one or two pieces of debris would steer the mind towards perceiving the larger abstracted textured pattern representing the rest of the debris as intended.

After painting a few days in Mid-City, we were ready to venture to Lakeview, where we knew the devastation was much worse. It was as though we were mountain climbers with Mid-City as our base camp, and now we were ready to attack the summit. Our destination was the breach in the 17th Street Canal, which was one of two primary sources of the flood devastation we had been painting in Mid-City many miles away. As we exited from I-10 onto West End Boulevard heading towards the Lakefront, we passed several mountainous trash piles, each as big as a city block and about thirty feet high. There were rows of trucks loading and unloading, backhoes and bulldozers moving around and on top of the piles, and makeshift observation towers around the perimeter. Seeing the scale of this operation firsthand gave me a deeper appreciation of the extent of the damage to my city.

We entered the neighborhood adjacent to the 17th Street Canal breach. The devastation was far worse here than in Mid-City. Wood-frame houses were swept off their foundations. Cars were sitting on top of fences. There was churned-up wreckage that was unidentifiable. There were all sorts of personal items that had been washed out of houses, although it was impossible to tell which house had generated what debris. The worst damage extended out about three or four blocks from the breach. At the breach, the velocity of the water had been much higher. As the water spread out away from the breach, its velocity slowed considerably.

As I walked around to survey where I was going to paint, I felt that my presence here was even more invasive than in Mid-City. I thought that perhaps if I had not spent time at my Mid-City base camp, I would not have the stomach for this.

There were many more National Guardsmen and relief workers, and I couldn't imagine why they didn't run us off, but they didn't. I remember thinking that photographers are in the enviable position of being able to quickly dart into a place they are not supposed to be, shoot a couple of rolls of film, and get out. Being a plein-air painter, it takes me hours just to set up and do one painting. This makes me much more vulnerable to the authorities. Also, I must choose my subjects more carefully. I will have so few paintings to say what needs to be said about all of this.

Here I was torn between my desire to document and my purer painterly motives. I looked at a house that had been swept off its foundation, with the base of the house in the foreground and the house itself in the background. It was very dramatic; a painting of this could say so much about the horrific event. However, I found the architecture of the house uninteresting. But perhaps I should reach, I thought . . . there's got to be some aesthetic richness I can grab onto here somewhere. This is the kind of internal dialog I often had in this neighborhood.

After painting a few days by the 17th Street Canal breach, we were ready for a change. We drove to the Municipal Yacht Basin and Southern Yacht Club, on Lake Pontchartrain. There we found that the storm surge and strong north winds had heaped large sailing yachts on top of each other in piles. Boats were now beached on dry land often as much as 200 yards away from the water. The Southern Yacht Club was also in ruins, burned from a rupture in a gas main during the flooding. While the force of nature here was perhaps even more devastating and powerful than anything we had seen thus far, there was some respite from the grim intrusiveness and uneasiness I felt in the neighborhoods. Here there were no broken lives, or at least there didn't seem to be, just multitudes of broken boats. And were they beautiful! We could now say things to each other such as, "Wow, man, look at this—this is really neat," without feeling as though we were

desecrating a grave. Perhaps much of the guilt I had been experiencing in the neighborhoods all along was because deep down I had felt, as I did here at the yacht basin, like a kid in a candy shop. Artistically these things we saw were so beautiful. When one sees a nineteenth-century naturalist painting of a ship wrecked on an iceberg, there is death and destruction, but there is also a higher beauty in the power of nature and the human drama.

As we searched for vantage points, clambering over debris, walking under and around precariously balanced boat hulls, with moving cranes in close proximity lifting yachts onto flatbed trucks, again I was struck at how accessible it all was to us. I believe that if any one of these places we had been painting had been the only scene of destruction in the city, it would have been barricaded and guarded and entry prohibited to the public. But in this case, devastation was so widespread that it was impossible to gather the resources to control the public, and there was little precedent to determine how to do so and if it should be done. This worked to our advantage.

For days we had the benefit of painting yachts as they are seldom seen. I've always loved the shapes of boat hulls. Their designs have been improvised so much throughout the millennia by trial and error that their present shapes were formed more by nature than by man. Seeing them now from underneath, on their sides, and from all sorts of other vantage points was quite a treat. And each painting I did of these boats in such odd dispositions evoked a sense of the powerful force that put them there.

By the time we received word that certain parts of the Lower Ninth Ward were being opened to the public, I had resolved the internal conflicts between my artistic motives and the need to demonstrate my sadness for all the pain and misery Katrina had inflicted on my beloved city. It would be OK to feel artistically elated on the inside, as long as it was coupled with quiet respect.

The Ninth Ward is a largely residential neighborhood

located downriver from the center of town. It is divided by the Industrial Shipping Canal, which connects the Mississippi River to Lake Pontchartrain. The downriver section is called the Lower Ninth Ward. St. Claude Avenue and North Claiborne Avenue are the two main roads that access the Lower Ninth Ward from downtown New Orleans. Both cross the Industrial Canal into the Lower Ninth Ward via drawbridges. St. Claude crosses the canal closer to the river. North Claiborne crosses the canal closer to the lake.

Neighborhoods on both sides of the canal were initially flooded in the early hours of the hurricane when the storm surge topped the canal levee and flood wall. During this flooding, the greatest loss of life and property happened when a river barge tore away from its moorings and slammed into the flood wall on the Lower Ninth side of the canal. This knocked out 200 yards of the flood wall just on the lake side of North Claiborne and sent a wall of water roaring into the neighborhood.

Diego and I arrived in the Lower Ninth Ward to witness the effects of this event some two and a half months after it happened. The North Claiborne bridge was closed to traffic, so we entered via the St. Claude bridge. We turned off of St. Claude and began to make our way through passable neighborhood streets towards North Claiborne. At first glance, the damage in the neighborhood close to St. Claude seemed no worse than in Mid-City. There was little visible structural damage, and the waterline on the houses only seemed to be approximately four feet above street level. We later found out that the floodwater in this area was up to the rooflines for a short time and then receded to about four feet, where it remained stagnant for a very long time. There was more and more visible property damage the closer we got to North Claiborne. In fact, North Claiborne seemed to be the line of demarcation separating severe damage from total devastation. At North Claiborne we saw houses that were swept off their foundations and piled into each other like a logjam.

One house had been broken in half around a telephone pole. There were roofs that had become detached from collapsed houses and were swept across North Claiborne.

For now this would be the farthest we could journey towards the source of the devastation. The most decimated part of the Lower Ninth, the area on the lake side of North Claiborne, was still barricaded. Emergency workers were still finding bodies there.

For about three weeks we painted along North Claiborne, often capturing the views down the cross streets into the barricaded areas. The views down these streets were surreal. As far as the eye could see there were piles of debris, crumpled wreckage, and broken houses. I feel that my paintings were more emotionally charged, knowing that so many people died there. It's always helped me artistically to feel a little off balance and ill at ease when painting. I've felt this way occasionally when I paint in places where there is a high crime rate. Perhaps it makes painting feel like a matter of life and death, as though I'm a Delta Force commando on a dangerous mission. Here I had this feeling, even though there was no crime. Each day that we came to the Lower Ninth to paint, part of me was looking forward to it and the other part was dreading it. Even though we had been slowly acclimating to progressively more terrible subjects, it seemed that it would be impossible to get used to this. I didn't know if I wanted to become used to it.

It was helpful to me that it was deserted there most of the time, except for the police and National Guard. There were not many neighborhood residents around at first, and the ones who were beginning to return for visits did not seem as distraught as I thought they would be. I must have had some idea that the Lower Ninth would be filled with people wailing and crying up into the heavens over their incomprehensible losses. I did witness a few emotional outbursts, especially from older people who had so much of their lives invested here. One lady started crying when she saw that I was painting the house in which her friend died. However, most of the people I spoke to seemed to have hardened up, at least on the outside, in the weeks, now months, since Katrina struck. In fact, some younger people appeared to be in good spirits and seemed to wear this tragedy that had befallen them like a badge of honor. I felt a little more at ease and less like having to walk on tiptoes while going about my business.

However, I always had to watch my behavior. This place was so inspiring that I thought my head was going to burst, but outwardly I had to remain quiet and austere. One day the unthinkable happened. A middle-aged man who saw me painting pulled his car over and expressed to me, "This is just so terrible." Inexplicably, my emotional armor cracked. "Yes, very sad," I replied, "but it's also *beautiful* in a way." My unbridled id had spewed forth like magma from a volcano! "There is nothing beautiful here," he abruptly and angrily retorted, and he drove away. He must have thought that I was a ghoul. I thought of doctors, journalists, firefighters, and other professionals whose jobs are at least in some part involved in human misery. How could a career firefighter who loves his job not think that fires are beautiful, at least "in a way"? I know that the great nineteenth-century English landscape painter Joseph Turner did when he made a series of paintings of the burning of the houses of Parliament.

It was reassuring that most everyone, neighborhood residents included, seemed to like what Diego and I were doing. We provided them with some needed distraction. Normally I don't like for people to talk to me while I'm painting, but there was nothing normal about any of this. One gentleman showed me drawings he did during the evacuation. A couple of young guys wanted to explain their conspiracy theory about how the levee was blown intentionally. I took a few addresses to mail images of my paintings for keepsakes. My conversations were generally not too long, and I was able to get right back to work.

We got permission to go up on the North Claiborne bridge, which was closed to traffic, where we could paint aerial views of the decimated neighborhood. It's a rare opportunity in any situation here in south Louisiana to paint landscape from an aerial perspective. From the bridge we could see the barge that had crashed through the flood wall and drifted down the street, wiping out a row of houses before coming to rest against a school bus. From here I could see why the devastation was so much greater in this area than along the 17th Street Canal. First, the break in the flood wall here was much larger, allowing a more tumultuous flow of water. Second, there seemed to be mostly small, raised, wood-frame houses here, whereas near the 17th Street Canal there were mostly large, brick houses built on slabs, which were more fortified against the fast-moving water.

Eventually we were allowed access to this most devastated area. This was hallowed ground. I could not imagine that Dresden could have looked much worse than this. There is no doubt that even more bodies will continue to be found as the dense, chaotic wreckage is cleared away. At this writing there are still hundreds of people unaccounted for in Katrina-affected areas.

Most streets had been cleared and were passable despite the odd house or, in most cases, piece of a house projecting out into the road. Very few wood-frame houses in this area were still sitting on their piers. A few streets off the beaten path, less crucial as trucking routes for debris removal, were left just as they were when the floodwaters receded. These streets were impassable, with fine and coarse debris, such as whole houses, fragments of houses and their contents, downed telephone poles and power lines, upturned automobiles, etc. It was important to see these uncleared roads because you were seeing virgin, natural destruction that had not been altered by bulldozers. Along the cleared roads, the destruction seemed even greater because the bulldozers had pushed the debris in the road onto the sidewalk, crushing and compressing it into the debris that was already there.

Closer to the break in the flood wall, where the water velocity had been greater, the devastation was more severe. In fact, the area within about two hundred to three hundred yards of the break consisted of nothing but bare slabs and fine debris, save for an occasional upturned car or truck.

The more intimate close-up views were even more tragic than the big panoramic views. These close-up views were more evocative of the real human catastrophe. Here you saw personal items. It was amazing to me how many family photos were in view in the mud, half-covered in dried silt. I tried not to look at them. There were so many of them, as though Katrina had searched them out by design. Relief workers and/or visiting neighborhood residents would frequently root out a child's toy such as a teddy bear and place it by the foundation of a house. When I first saw this I thought it was an accident, but it happened too often for this to be the case. Presumably they were made as shrines to lost innocence. I decided to stick to the bigger view, not because I couldn't stand to look at these more intimate views, but because I found the expansive, churned-up vistas more compelling. Never in my paintings, though, have the textured patterns and flecks of paint that abstract the little details of the scene carried such a profound meaning.

It was getting into winter when we began to paint in this inner sanctum of destruction. The bare, skeletal trees seemed to lend themselves more to the nature of this place. The more we painted here, the more at ease I felt. I began to see these crushed houses less as representing tombs and broken lives and more as graceful voices speaking about the force of nature.

Painting in the aftermath of Katrina has provided some extraordinary artistic challenges. Since I have spent so much of my career painting architecture in its pristine state, it is quite an opportunity to see and paint it when it has been so ravaged by the forces of nature, splayed inside out. At first the collapse of a house seemed chaotic and random. Try to paint it that way

Collapsed houses on Tennessee Street between North Tonti and North Galvez. 12" x 16". Painting by Diego Larguia.

and you won't succeed. It's amazing how much order and poetry there is in it and how much we know subconsciously about things like this that we seldom, if ever, see.

In the best of times, New Orleans architecture has a natural waviness and organic quality to it, due to the soil subsidence and humidity. This took on a new meaning in the Lower Ninth. Many houses had become buoyant and were transported by the rising floodwater, eventually coming to rest on top of smaller but denser objects such as cars and foundations or porches of other houses. They often looked like large serpents that had slithered over and settled on these things. The framing of the house and its roof supports were the serpent's ribs and back, and the twisted and buckled vinyl weatherboards were its skin. Plastic siding has never been so beautiful! There was so much movement and gesture in many of the houses that were left standing that sometimes it looked

as though they were dancing. I saw a house that was swept off its foundation and pushed against its tall iron security fence. Its pillarless overhang drooped over the fence, as though the house was a prisoner trying to escape but just didn't have the energy to do it. I was brought back to cold reality when I saw a neighborhood resident, wearing her Red Cross-issued Hazmat suit and dust mask, stooping down to pick up a piece of a plate or small knickknack from where her house used to be. She must not know how beautiful this place is to me as an artist . . . at least for now.

After February I thought that I was finished painting hurricane destruction. It was wearing on me and it was a good place to stop. I had successfully completed thirty paintings and had business obligations out of town for the months of March and April. Having initially thought that New Orleans' art market was going to be as devastated as its neighborhoods, I had made arrangements with the galleries that represent me in Jacksonville and Atlanta to do some plein-air painting in their regions during this period. I was determined to keep to my word, even though the art market in New Orleans was recovering much better than I had anticipated. The change did me good. It was refreshing to get away from all my worries for a while, and I produced some good work.

When I returned to New Orleans, I had no desire to continue painting Lower Ninth Ward scenes of destruction. I wanted to paint ordinary neighborhood scenes in the Uptown area where I lived. Now, some eight months after Katrina, the older sections of New Orleans by the river bore little evidence of the storm's impact. There were some exceptions to this, such as the occasional blue tarp on a roof, but for the most part it looked normal. In fact, it was even more lively than before Katrina, because a larger population had been compressed into this more habitable part of town.

Artistically, I had been carrying some extra baggage while documenting the storm destruction. I am not a journalist of historical events by trade. Over the last couple of decades, I have become more and more interested in using my painting to explore the mechanics of human vision. I believe that advancing our understanding of human vision is the only way to advance visual art. There are so many interesting visual phenomena to explore with painting. My favorite is the first principle of Gestalt, which I mentioned earlier. Even though we know that an object has not changed, that the light on it has not changed, and that our vantage point has not changed, the appearance of the object is constantly changing depending upon how we scan it with our eyes. There are so many other instances where physics conflicts with psychophysics. For example, it is a fact that the sky on a clear day is a more saturated blue straight above your head than it is anywhere close to the horizon (physics). But because at least half of the neurons that detect color differences do so at boundaries between different colors, there is a place closer to the horizon where the sky *seems* to be a richer blue than it is straight above your head (psychophysics).

To tackle such quandaries as this, I have sought out ordinary subjects to paint. I believe that you are made more aware of the pure sensation of seeing if the subject matter is not innately interesting. In my scenes of Lower Ninth Ward destruction, the subject matter is so dominant that it is easy to be impressed more by the subject than by the seeing of it. This is why I have made a practice of painting ordinary things as much as possible. I have certainly made exceptions. If you live and paint in a place like New Orleans, there is too much majesty not to succumb to it occasionally. Many of my pre-Katrina paintings selected for this book attest to this. These majestic sights were what originally hooked me on landscape painting so many years ago. But most days I find myself on an ordinary neighborhood street taking in a view from close up or far away, wondering what visual cues will make you see and understand this the way I do.

However, in the weeks following my return, I had great difficulty maintaining my routine. I would reconnoiter a neighborhood as I had always done before Katrina. Something would grab my interest, and I would set up and begin to paint. Very quickly, though, I would lose interest in the subject, and the painting would become a forced study, devoid of any poetry. This happened painting after painting. In two months of painting every day, I had only three successes. As much as I knew in my rational mind what I had to do and how important it was, my gut was telling me that it was unimportant. I was thinking about other things and talking to myself while painting.

I explored several possible reasons for this affliction. First, I considered that I might have been emotionally and physically tired from the rigors of the past year. Maybe I was just resting now. I also thought that I might have become a drama junkie, having spent so much time painting those horrific scenes of destruction. Perhaps my ability to be captivated by subtlety had atrophied. And what about my righteous indignation? One of my greatest motivations to paint has been my anger at the representational art community's general lack of interest in the actual visual experience. It's ironic that so few visual artists seem to care anything about vision these days. I have worked in my laboratory like a mad scientist to create the perfect statement that will show them just how wrong they are! Anger has always fueled me. Now, I was more complacent and less angry. The only anger I seemed to be able to muster was reserved for my insurance company. Also, and perhaps most importantly, painting in this less affected part of town felt a bit insincere. Once, when painting a house on St. Charles Avenue, I had a flashback to my childhood. I remembered standing in line at the Haunted House at Disney World and being amazed by its beautiful neo-gothic facade. It looked just like a haunted house. When I got up close, though, I could see through some young pine trees that were supposed to block my view of an expansive corrugated-metal building behind the facade. Was I painting in Disney World now? Could my very choice of subject constitute a lie?

In my rational mind I understood my artistic objectives and knew where I needed to be and what I needed to do, but I still felt a calling, one that I had been ignoring. I felt like a first-round draft choice sitting on the sidelines of a very important game. Within a week, a call from Pelican Publishing Company proposing that I do this book provided the catalyst that I needed to once again venture away from the river into the flood-damaged areas of town. This time, though, I would not overtly look for hurricane themes. I would just be in these places and paint whatever presented itself and was artistically compelling. In this way I could pursue my artistic objectives but also feel that I was not hiding from the truth about my home.

Thus began a new body of Katrina paintings. Rather than explore the horrific scenes of devastation caused by fast-moving water, as I did in most of the first thirty paintings, this next body of work would have as its subject the houses and neighborhoods affected by the slow-rising floodwater and the impact of high wind and rain. This was the most common subject that could be seen throughout 80 percent of New Orleans. Having started this body of work almost a year after Katrina, I would capture the somewhat more subtle continuum of repair and rebuilding on the one hand and of neglect and reclamation by nature on the other.

Exploring these areas, I found many sights that provided great narratives about the disposition of New Orleans but that were not interesting to me artistically. For example, in Lakeview there were houses that had been renovated so perfectly that they looked like new constructions, complete with sodded yards and "for sale" signs. These houses were often surrounded by blighted houses that still had visible waterlines, trees atop roofs, and yards overgrown with weeds and cat's-claw, untouched since Katrina. Such neighborhood streets looked like surreal movie sets. I wondered who would want to buy such a perfect house and lawn in this place. I tried to picture kids playing in the yard and

Dad barbecuing. As amazing as these sights were, I had no desire to paint them.

I had more artistic success in a small subdivision close to the lake and just east of the London Avenue Canal. This area consisted largely of small, wood-frame bungalows. Just a few scattered houses were being raised about eight or ten feet above the other houses in the neighborhood. I painted a view of one such house. The original columns for the porch seemed to have been recklessly broken and were suspended in the air unsupported. The house had been raised to its final height and was temporarily resting on four stacks of railroad ties assembled like Lincoln Logs (this seems to be the most common technique used by shoring companies). The permanent piers were being made with cinder blocks. The house loomed majestically above the surrounding houses as it was being fortified against nature. The construction crew was not working that day, but the lone FEMA trailer and parked vehicle in this neighborhood of mostly blighted houses demonstrated a defiant pioneer spirit. The scene was beautifully lit, with the sun hitting hard on one side of the house and trailer and glancing on the other. The buildings of the University of New Orleans (UNO) could be seen on the horizon.

There is talk among certain neighborhood groups of covering with siding the tall piers of houses being raised, to make the houses more visually pleasing. I hope they reconsider. Exposing the piers (as was done in our historical raised Greek Revival cottages) is more beautiful. Instead of shamefully hiding our situation, it proudly shows our respect for and struggle against nature. We have a saying in the art world: "form follows function." In time, people will become acclimated to the sight of these exposed piers and an aesthetic precedent will have been set.

In this same vicinity, a little closer to the lake and the London Avenue Canal, there is another subdivision composed only of two-story, wood-frame houses. The only aspect of these houses that keeps them from being identical "cook-

MID-CITY DOUGHBOY, TULANE AVENUE AT SOUTH GALVEZ STREET, JULY 2006. 12" X 12". ELEVEN MONTHS AFTER KATRINA STRUCK, THE DIRTY WATERLINE DENOTING THE LEVEL OF THE FLOODWATER COULD STILL BE SEEN ON THE PEDESTAL. I WAS TAKEN BY THIS VIEW BECAUSE, FROM THIS ANGLE, IT SEEMED THAT THE DOUGHBOY WAS CHEERING THE CITY ON TO RECOVERY. IRONICALLY, WHEN SEEN FROM THE SIDE, HE IS ACTUALLY THROWING A GRENADE!

ie cutters" is that the roofs are of different designs and pitches and oriented in different directions. I later learned that these houses were originally made as two-family dwellings (upper/lower) to house military personnel and their families when the site of UNO was a naval air station during World War II. Some of the houses were being renovated in small clusters, but there was a majestic view of a swath of these houses, blighted and overgrown with weeds, receding away into the distance, one after another. They were set into a landscape cluttered with dead trees. There were other interesting elements in the foreground, such as a wrecked foundation of a house and a scrap of blue tarp. The day I painted this view there was a broken overcast sky with one cumulus cloud in the far distance catching the direct sunlight. Keying the rest of the painting a little lower to accommodate this sunlit cloud added to the overall eerie effect. If not for the architecture, which was atypical for New Orleans, this view would have signified better than anything the enormity of the damage to so much of New Orleans.

Broadmoor is a neighborhood about a five-minute drive from my house, closer to the river than Mid-City but flooded even worse since it is lower. When first venturing out to paint hurricane destruction, Diego and I had driven through Broadmoor on our way to Mid-City. Broadmoor became the neighborhood I connected with the most since painting in the Lower Ninth Ward. There are narrow, intimate streets such as Vincennes Place filled with beautiful little cottages. There are larger streets such as Jefferson Avenue, which is architecturally eclectic, but most of the houses seem to be from the 1920s and 1930s when no building expense was spared. I encountered a large variety of flora, which had become overgrown around blighted houses. The older, larger crape myrtle trees had survived the flood but seemed to be distressed. The younger, smaller ones had died but were quite beautiful in that state, with their gnarly bundles of twigs partially occluding my view of the houses.

Twice while painting in Broadmoor I got to observe and record restoration work being done on houses. In one of these instances I was captivated by a large view of houses on both sides of a street at an intersection. On one side of the street there was the industry of recovery. The houses were clean and being renovated and had FEMA trailers parked in front of them. On the other side of the street was a house that had been completely neglected, save for a tarp on the roof, which had become tattered and discolored over the past year. It had been a beautiful old two-story house with extravagant woodwork. Katrina had dealt it a terrific blow, which had been exacerbated by neglect. Though it still had good bones, bits and pieces of it had fallen off, and it had become overgrown with weeds. My initial concept was to make a painting of the bigger view, contrasting the rebuilding on one side of the street with the neglect on the other. As I was laying in the underpainting, though, I began to notice activity around the blighted house. What an incredible coincidence! It had been a year since Katrina and renovations were beginning on this house at the very moment that I was starting a painting of it. Unfortunately, the painting I attempted that morning was to be a failure. With all the activity around this *formerly* blighted house, it was becoming more and more difficult for me to keep my eyes moving around the bigger view. Vehicles were coming and going, and workers were removing drywall and furniture and dumping it into the street. I struggled on with the painting, but my distraction away from the whole, and the conflict between my initial perception of the house and the different, more overpowering perception of it that I now had, eventually got the best of me. I returned the next morning with the clear objective to make a painting that focused only on this house and the sidewalk and road in front of it. It was just as busy around the house as on the previous day, but the view was even more dramatic because the piles of debris had grown both in size and variety.

Better attuned to the subject, and with an added sense of urgency I often feel after a failure, I succeeded with this painting. Just as I was applying the last strokes of paint, the debris removal crew working for the city arrived with their front-loader and made short work of the piles. These cleanup crews usually come through a neighborhood about once a month. They just happened to be in the area this day. The street was clean by the time I finished packing up. It was as though a flower had briefly blossomed for me and then was gone. As I had stood there painting for so long, I was observing all the while the activities around this house and the neighborhood rhythms, such as the periodic dumping of debris from the house and even the competing "meals on wheels" trucks driving by at certain intervals, each with its distinct pattern of horn honking, all of which were embellished by the melodic sound of Latino music coming from the house. I believe that this kind of knowledge, gathered over time, increases the depth and richness of the succinct statements that I make about these experiences.

Perhaps time is the crucial ingredient. I believe that the most profound statement an artist can make is in the place where he lives. It is too easy to find inspiration far away from home. When I am traveling and painting in different places, everything seems so fresh and new. But the newness is usually on the surface. When you've recorded all the different surface qualities, you have to look a bit deeper to keep the game interesting. Incubating over a long time in the place where you live results in a more profound statement. The flashy international rock stars and shock jocks of journalism and photojournalism stormed through our region in the wake of Katrina, gathering material for their best-selling books and movies, often marginalizing our equally talented but lesser-known local artisans. When the newness of it faded away, so did they. This more subtle, extended period of recovery is of no interest to them. It will be up to the artists who live here and love this place to patiently sit with it and record all of its changing nuances as it recovers.

Katrina caused me to temporarily diverge from my artistic course, to paint the most dramatic subjects I have ever seen. I don't know if I will ever be able to observe and make a painting of a wood-frame house again without being aware of how it would look if ravaged by the forces of nature, and how easy it is for that to happen. I believe that everyone's point of view should be so altered. If New Orleans is to survive and thrive in the third millennium, it is important that we appreciate how beautiful and fragile it is.

Dauphine Street between St. Ferdinand and Port streets. 18" x 24".

Houses on Eleonore between Benjamin and Hurst streets. 22" x 20".

View from the corner of Patton and Calhoun streets. 12" x 12".

Solara and white rocking chairs, Laurel Street between Arabella and Nashville. 16" x 20".

Maple Street close to Cherokee Street. 16" x 20". Much of the canvas is devoted to the large, gas-guzzling, view-obstructing Chevy Suburban!

JOSEPH STREET AT PITT STREET. 11" X 14" THIS WAS A ONE-HOUR DEMONSTRA-
TION FOR MY LANDSCAPE PAINTING CLASS. SUCH A SUCCESS AS THIS REAFFIRMS
THAT NO AMOUNT OF METICULOUS RENDERING CAN COMPETE WITH A VERY
SIMPLE BUT STRONG STATEMENT OF THE WHOLE.

Fountain in Audubon Park. 28" x 22".

JOGGER WITH HER DOG. 16" X 20".

WET PAVEMENT AROUND FOUNTAIN. 20" X 16".

Longue Vue House and Gardens. 16" x 20".

Rose in the gardens at Longue Vue House and Gardens. 14" x 11".

Opposite left: Spiral staircase at Longue Vue House and Gardens. 30" x 15".

Opposite right: Rose arbor. Prytania Street close to Henry Clay. 20" x 10".

At Right: Sidewalk along Josephine Street close to Magazine Street. 14" x 11".

Victorian house on Palmer Avenue close to Loyola Avenue, on an overcast day. 16" x 20".

Same house as on opposite page, in afternoon sunlight. 16" x 20".

The Rink shopping center. Prytania and Washington. 15" x 30".

Greek Revival mansion. St. Charles
Avenue at Fourth Street. 20" x 16".

INTERSECTION OF MAGAZINE STREET AND LOUISIANA AVENUE. 16" X 20".

Uglesich's Restaurant, Baronne and Erato. 15" x 30".

Oretha Castle Haley Boulevard between Felicity and Euterpe. 15" x 30".

Oretha Castle Haley Boulevard between Euterpe and Terpsichore. 20" x 16".

Lee Circle. 20" x 16".

New Orleans Criminal Courts Building. 15" x 30". In the best of times. New Orleans has had considerable urban blight outside its tourist areas. If you didn't know better, you might think from the ruined framework of the sign shown in the upper right corner of this painting that this view is from after Katrina rather than before.

S & M Iron Works, corner of Mandeville
and Dauphine streets. 11" x 14".

Saints Peter and Paul Catholic Church, corner of Mandeville and Burgundy streets. 20" x 16".

Corner of Constance and Josephine. 16" x 20".

Huey Long Bridge. 16" x 20".

*TREE BLOWN OVER BY HURRICANE CINDY, AUDUBON PARK
(A FORESHADOWING OF KATRINA). 15" X 30".*

Lake Pontchartrain, near the University of New Orleans. 22" x 28".

Barge cranes docked on the Mississippi River behind Audubon Zoo. 18" x 24".

Flooded cars in Mid-City. 15" x 30".

Houses along the 17th Street Canal. 15" x 30".

RUINS OF SIDMAR'S. 18" X 24". THE CEMENT PIERS SEEN IN THE FOREGROUND OF THE PAINTING WERE ALL THAT WAS LEFT OF THE VENERABLE OLD SEAFOOD RESTAURANT.

Sloops in the road, Municipal Yacht Basin. 16" x 20". The receding floodwaters deposited these two boats on land, precariously balanced on their keels and leaning against each other.

BEACHED BOATS. MUNICIPAL YACHT BASIN. 10" X 20".

PILE OF YACHTS, NEAR THE SOUTHERN YACHT CLUB. 10" X 20". CREATED BY THE STORM SURGE, THIS PILE OF LARGE SAILING YACHTS (MANY WERE TWO MASTED) WAS EVEN LARGER BEFORE I MADE THIS PAINTING. AT LEAST TWO YACHTS HAD ALREADY BEEN REMOVED FROM THE TOP OF THE PILE BY SALVAGERS.

SLOOP IN THE PARKING LOT OF THE SOUTHERN YACHT CLUB. 10" X 20".

Lower Ninth Ward, twisted flat-bottom boat under the St. Claude Bridge. 18" x 18". Fast-rising floodwater piled up against the upramp of the bridge and was funneled through the car tunnels (shown in the middle ground of the painting) as if through the floodgates of a dam.

North Claiborne bridge. 11" x 14".

Lower Ninth Ward neighborhood seen from the North Claiborne bridge. 18" x 24".

BREACH IN THE INDUSTRIAL CANAL AND RIVER BARGE
SEEN FROM THE NORTH CLAIBORNE BRIDGE. 15" X 30".

Disheveled houses on Forstall between North Claiborne and North Derbigny. 15" x 30".

Lower Ninth Ward barricaded street, view down Reynes Street from
North Claiborne. 15" x 30". (New Orleans Museum of Art)

House broken around telephone pole.
North Claiborne and Forstall. 18" x 24".

HOUSES ALONG REYNES BETWEEN NORTH
DERBIGNY AND NORTH ROMAN. 15" X 30".

FOUNDATION OF HOUSE AND CRUSHED CAR, TENNESSEE CLOSE TO NORTH PRIEUR. 15" X 30". (THE HISTORIC NEW ORLEANS COLLECTION)

Debris field, Lizardi and North Johnson. 15" x 30".

Houses smashed into each other, North Galvez between Andry and Choctaw. 18" x 24". Brick houses built on slabs usually stayed in place, while raised, wood-frame houses were swept away in the fast-moving floodwaters. Here the wood-frame house could go no farther after it collided with the brick house and the car. It broke open and contents such as the sofa spilled out over the hood of the car. As surreal as this scene was, it was made even more eerie by the beautiful dappled sunlight that illuminated it the day that I made this painting.

*House slumping over security fence.
Forstall between North Tonti and
North Rocheblave. 15" x 30".*

HOUSE ON TOP OF F-150 TRUCK, TENNESSEE BETWEEN NORTH TONTI AND NORTH GALVEZ. 15" X 30". ON THE OPPOSITE PAGE IS A SEPARATE PAINTING OF A CLOSE-UP VIEW OF THIS SCENE DONE ON AN OVERCAST DAY. THE OVERCAST SKY PROVIDED A MORE EVEN LIGHT SO THAT THE EPICENTER OF THIS EVENT COULD BE BETTER EXAMINED. ON THE DAYS THAT I PAINTED HERE, THREE DIFFERENT PASSERSBY INDEPENDENTLY REMARKED THAT THE F-150 TRUCK REMINDED THEM OF THE WICKED WITCH OF THE EAST.

House on top of F-150 truck (close-up). 18" x 24".

Collapsed house and car. North Galvez and Forstall. 10" x 20".

Tattered fence, Reynes between North Tonti and North Rocheblave. 15" x 30".

VIEW FROM THE CORNER OF FORSTALL
AND NORTH ROCHEBLAVE. 15" X 30".

VIEW FROM FORSTALL AND NORTH ROCHEBLAVE.
BRIDGE IN BACKGROUND. 15" X 30".

Fragment of yellow house on top of red car. North Tonti and Reynes. 15" x 30".

Debris field with steps of house and cars, Tennessee between North Galvez and North Prieur. 15" x 30". Initially, I set up my easel in front of the steps of the house shown in the painting, using the steps to set down some of my equipment. As I began to paint, though, I realized that what I saw from this vantage point was indistinguishable from an ordinary junkyard. Backing up a bit to include the steps in the foreground of the painting provided just the visual cue that was needed to portray this place.

Early morning fog, Tricou at North Rocheblave. 15" x 30".

Opposite top: Boat cradled in telephone lines. Tennessee between North Tonti and North Dorgenois. 10" x 20".

Opposite bottom: Yellow house crushed into van and tree. 12" x 36". This was the last painting that I did in the Lower Ninth Ward and the only one for which I do not know the location. For all the other paintings I diligently recorded the locations using a GPS as I painted them (most of the street signs had been washed away by the floodwater). I didn't have time to establish the location of this scene the day I painted it and I did not return to the Lower Ninth Ward for many months. When I did, I could find no trace of this scene.

NEW ORLEANS ONE YEAR AFTER KATRINA

VIEW FROM THE CORNER OF LAPEYROUSE AND NORTH JOHNSON STREETS.
15" X 30". I WAS STRUCK BY THIS VIEW BECAUSE THE CATHOLIC ARCHITECTURE
(I BELIEVE A SCHOOL AND ITS CHAPEL) IN THE DISTANCE LOOMING OVER THE
WIND- AND FLOOD-DAMAGED NEIGHBORHOOD EVOKED A SENSE OF HOPE
RISING UP ABOVE DESPAIR.

House in the process of being raised. Wingate Drive between Burbank Drive and Robert E. Lee Boulevard. 15" x 30". The University of New Orleans is seen in the distance. (Louisiana State Museum)

Wrecked lighthouse seen from the parking lot of the Southern Yacht Club. 15" x 30". In the immediate aftermath of Katrina, the lighthouse was listing to one side but still standing, its ground floor severely damaged. Eventually the ground floor collapsed, as shown in my painting.

Blighted houses along Warrington Drive close to the London Avenue Canal. 15" x 30". The houses in this painting are actually seen from the rear, close to the intersection of Leon C. Simon Drive and Waldo Drive.

Construction crew working on house. Upperline close to South Johnson. 15" x 30". (Louisiana State Museum)

HOUSE IN THE PROCESS OF BEING GUTTED. CORNER
OF SOUTH GAYOSO AND GENERAL PERSHING. 11" X 14".

Abandoned house, corner of South Miro and Upperline streets. 15" x 30". One year after Katrina, many homes in flood-damaged neighborhoods appeared on the surface to be normal. If not for a sign on the front door of this house that said, "Looters will be cursed" (too small for my clumsy big brushes to articulate), the view shown in this painting could have been from before Katrina.

Vincennes Place at South Tonti. 15" x 30".

Vincennes Place between South Rocheblave and South Tonti. 15" x 30".

FRONT-LOADER AND RAISED HOUSE. VINCENNES PLACE BETWEEN SOUTH ROCHEBLAVE AND SOUTH TONTI. 16" X 20".

ABANDONED, OVERGROWN HOUSE WITH DEAD CRAPE
MYRTLE TREES, ROBERT CLOSE TO SOUTH JOHNSON.
12" X 24".

Octavia Street between South Tonti and South Rocheblave streets. 15" x 30".

STATE STREET DRIVE CLOSE TO SOUTH TONTI. 15" X 30".